Table of

BOSS THOSE NERVES!
Overcoming Stage Fright, Performance Anxiety, Competition and Presentation Nerves.

This book is for anyone who has to do anything in the way of performing: playing music, singing, acting, dancing, sports, presentation, and public speaking. It's to help you with that amazing journey to give of your best.

Performance anxiety, performance stress, nerves, stage fright....call it what you will. It can get in the way – but it doesn't have to! Here are some top tips to help you turn it to your advantage.

(By the way, and just in case it confuses you, we use different versions of spelling for the verb practise, and the noun practice in the UK.)

CHAPTER ONE
Know that you are not alone

Does it seem to you as though everyone else goes out there, looks so poised, and delivers their best without fear or trembling? Don't be fooled!

You never know what journey somebody has been on to get to where they are. You never know what is going on inside their heads and hearts.

Historically, many people didn't like to talk about it, thinking it is a sign of weakness, or that people will think that they are just not cut out to be performers. Some people almost think it is catching!! Happily, in these enlightened days more people have 'come out' about it, and anyone worth their salt within the performing professions (I mean producers, directors, coaches etc etc) knows that it can be worked with and overcome.[1]

Many great performers are well known to experience performance anxiety, sometimes to a severe degree. The famous classical actor, Laurence Olivier often felt like he was choking, or was physically sick before performing. Maureen Lipman says she nearly didn't make it to the Olivier awards because of nerves. Michael Gambon, Benedict Cumberbatch, Dame Maggie Smith, Andrea Bocelli, Rhianna, Barbara Streisand, Beyoncé, Adele, Katy Perry, Jonas Kaufmann, Ella Fitzgerald[2], Mikhail Baryshnikov, Jurgen Klopp[3], Glenn Hall, have all suffered its effects. The list goes on and on. Just listen to some victory interviews during the Olympics, and you will hear lots of athletes mention their nerves.

Performance nerves can come and go. Some days will feel OK, while on others, you might want to run away. I recall one respected psychologist, who specialises in the field, saying that he thought performers who say they have never had stage fright or 'nerves' are lying, either to you or to themselves. In other words: performance anxiety is perfectly NORMAL.

CHAPTER TWO

Preparation, preparation, preparation!..........Then accept where you are

You wouldn't expect to go into the boxing ring to fight a world champion boxer without training up, would you? On the other hand, if you have trained well but just tire yourself out practising, you wouldn't do so well either.

So first, you need to know what you are aiming for when you practise. If you are an actor, is it to know your lines fluently? If you are a singer, to know the music and text, even in a foreign language? If you are a public speaker, is it to know your speech off by heart, or know what's in it well and then use notes? If you are a runner, to run your optimum race?

Then you need to understand what this really entails. It's best (and for a professional, a given) that you are well beyond the stage where you are 'thinking' what the next line or step is going to be, or having to count like mad for a musical entry, or being glued to your auto-cue. Why? Well, you want to interpret, don't you? Get inside the character, into their emotions, or get your message across strongly. If you are a singer or a musician, you will want to embody the music and deliver the composer's intentions, as well as display your individual flair. If you're a golfer, I would imagine that it would be better not to be altering your swing during the competition, but have it practised in. So that tells you the amount of preparation that you need. Practise until that fluency is automatic and you can immerse yourself in the important stuff.

And guess what? Recent neurotechnology[4] shows us that when you get into that fluent phase you start to use different parts of your brain from the bits that are used in the non-fluent phase.

Or, to put it another way: whilst you are still learning to ride a bike, you can't concentrate on where you are going, but when the bike riding becomes automatic, you can. That's because you won't be worrying about what you have to do to stay upright!

Remember, if you can't do your stuff reliably in the studio (i.e. during practice), or in training, you are not going to be able to do it reliably in performance. SO DON'T EXPECT TO!! No amount of wishing is going to magic that fact away.

And that brings us to the next bit......

Life sure ain't perfect, and we'd all like the ideal practice time, where life, mishaps, illness, or some other unforeseen issue didn't interrupt our best made plans. But it does! And the result is that preparation wise, we aren't always (or even often) where we would really like to be when it comes to the big day. So, no hoping for a miracle, no pleading to the stars above to correct that bit that goes wrong nine times out of ten. Just expect that little fault to be there and do the best you can even with it there. If you are plumb lucky it may go your way, but truly, get real and don't expect it. What do you want of fate, a special ticket?

And believe it or not, one can overdo the perfectionism! You are hardly going to do your best if you over-practise and are tired out physically and mentally, are you? Whether you are a high-level performer or just starting out, there is a point at which you need to stop. Anyone dedicated to their profession will aim for perfection, but it's unrealistic to think that this is a constantly achievable goal. In fact, the psychologist Andy Evans has found that those with the most successful careers often score lower on perfectionist traits than somewhat less successful performers![5]

So, my next helpful top tip is:

CHAPTER THREE

*Practise with your mistakes
and with chaos around you.*

Yes, you read it right. Things go wrong in live performance. That is what makes it exciting, thrilling and yes, sometimes damnably frustrating!! So, get to grips with this fact of life and work out how you are going to cope.

Whilst to get to any level, of course, one must make corrections and improvements over days, weeks, months and years, you also need to set some time aside for run throughs which are warts and all. I would suggest that you do this often after you have reached the fluent stage, but even in the learning stage you need to do it. Other advantages of doing this are so that you know where the mistakes are likely to be, and because you won't achieve fluency without it.

The main thing is that you know you can survive
and continue to the end!

When you make a mistake, practise not letting it show on the outside. Carry on with a smile like that bum note was the best bit of music or the best sound in the world, like that stumble was the most original bit of choreography ever. Do that when you practise and when it comes to performance you won't be fazed, and you can do the same. If you don't make a big deal out of it, the audience certainly won't (well there's always one! More of them later!!).

I say again, any performer knows that things go wrong in live performance. You just have to learn to deal with it and move on.

What if there is a distraction? There often is!! No, don't be a divo/diva and stomp out of the arena. You'd probably spend more time off stage than on! You need to get used to focusing DESPITE distractions.

Practise with unrelated and random noises in the background. Turn the accompaniment on and off again and see how you can carry on. Let the kids or your room-mates run riot around you. Play in the wrong shoes etc. etc. Get yourself to the mental place where a massive crashing noise could happen, and you could carry on undisturbed.

Remember, it doesn't have to be a perfect performance to be a great performance. The whole really is much greater than the sum of its parts. Just think back to some of the great performances and performers that you have seen and heard. You will find this to be very true.

CHAPTER FOUR

Who got out on the wrong side of the bed, then?

What I am talking about here is the fact that, in everyday life, on some days we just don't feel as great as on other days. Who knows why? The weather 's too hot, too cold, too overcast, our hormones, too much junk food, the dog woke us up too early, whatever. Maybe the bed felt particularly lumpy, or we had an odd dream, or we're just too excited about something. Whilst we must try and give ourselves the best conditions (more of which later), there are some things we just can't control.

Why then, do we performers expect, yes expect, that on big performance day, we will feel at our best and so perform at our best? Yep, we may be able to practise getting in the zone so that we get peak performance more often, but come on, it isn't going to happen every time. So, GET REAL and KNOW THAT!

But also know that, if you are a student, your regular practise and development is going to mean that this month, your worst day is going to be at least as good as your best day was six months ago. As time goes on and you are a more regular performer, your experience in general, or your familiarity with a piece, conductor or venue is going to have a similar effect. Either way, when you are practising, even when you are approaching performance, there will be some variation day to day.

So you need to come to terms with reality. The day of the performance really could be one of those 'less good' days. What you need to do is to get to a level where your 'worst' day in normal variation, whilst not your best, will be good enough to be acceptable. If you can't say that, maybe you should think twice about presenting it, or competing this time around.

5

Treat your symptoms with understanding. Then boss them!!

Well, what are the symptoms of stage fright/performance anxiety/performance nerves/performance stress?

You may experience some or all of these, and maybe a few others:

- Shaky knees and other wobbly bits.
- Stiffening up, a locked throat, arms, legs and other bits.
- Sweaty palms, sweaty anything.
- Racing or palpitating heart, thumping away in the chest.
- 'Butterflies' in the tummy.
- Feeling sick or actual vomiting.
- Loss of appetite.
- Dry mouth.
- Blurred vision.
- A need to visit the toilet frequently (pre-performance pee is a classic!).
- Feeling anxious, scared, overwhelmed, and in extreme cases, even terrified.
- A feeling that you can't get enough breath.
- A feeling of not really being there, or paradoxically, an excessively calm feeling.
- Thinking negative or distracting thoughts, an inability to focus, feeling your mind has gone or will go blank.
- Feeling you are out of control or feeling weak.

What the heck, you say?! Where did that lot come from?

Adrenaline, adrenaline, adrenaline!

Yes, it comes from adrenaline. The production of that exciting excitement hormone in our bodies is stimulated by a pathway through certain parts of the brain: namely the amygdala, the hypothalamus and the pituitary gland, which then sends a message to the adrenal glands saying 'all systems go!! Hey presto! Adrenaline is produced, and this stimulates a set of nerves called the sympathetic system that causes most of the effects listed above.

You may well have heard of the flight or fight (or freeze) response. It's thought to be a primal instinct from way back, which is related to survival – say fighting, fleeing from danger, or staying stock still so you are not found by a great animal or something in the forest. It's that millisecond ('cos that's all it takes), where you perceive a threat, and the old amygdala can go into full swing.

However, I think you would agree it is a bit over the top for saying a few lines, singing a few notes or dancing about a stage, or running along a track. (Of course, I am minimising, but you get my drift. We are not in an equivalent emergency life-threatening situation even if it feels like that sometimes).

But we can feel that we are being judged.........and we can think lots of other negative stuff. More of that later.... But for now.....

There is a good reason why that hormone is useful to us when performing. It makes us hyper-alert, ready, aware of our surroundings and what we must do. It allows us to react quickly, to be on top of our game. It's also a sign that you care. It's just a question of finding the balance, just the right amount.[5]

'How do I do that?' I hear you cry. Well here are a few suggestions. Pick the ones you think are most relevant to you and give them a try.

• *Adjust your attitude to the effects of adrenaline* •

If you think about it, some activities that are thrilling can give you many similar 'symptoms'. Remember how it felt on a roller-coaster ride when you enjoyed one, or how you felt before seeing someone you're in love with, or doing something you have wanted to do for ages, or how it felt when your team were winning or scored that goal, jumped off that diving board into the pool as a kid, or similar? It was great to feel your heart racing, that thumping of the heart, that slight tremble, wasn't it? So, what's the difference when we get the same symptoms in performance?

The difference is how we think about it. Try and view the positive sides of such a reaction and convert those feelings of fear to ones of excitement. Allow the symptoms and enjoy them as excited anticipation. You really can BOSS the way you think about that adrenaline.

• *Get rid of some* •

Sometimes, there's just too much adrenaline floating around, and we need to simply get rid of some. This we can do through exercise. Depending on how much you need to get rid of will determine how much you need to do. For some a 10 minute walk will do it, for others, a one mile run prior to performance is what is needed (truly), or you might like to do some star jumps in the dressing room, or just swing your arms about. If you're trembling, see how much you can get your body to 'shake it out'.

Experiment, and learn what is good for you. Yes, you can BOSS the amount of adrenaline in your body.

• And keep moving: •

Because your body is 'trying to' run away or fight, the muscles can sometimes tremble, but can also sometimes lock (often singers and speakers may feel stiff in the jaw or tongue, or larynx). Either way, it can be really helpful to keep your head, neck, shoulders moving, to loosen the jaw up and down. If you are a voice user, hum, or do a lip trill and a tongue trill or equivalent through your range and keep this going gently. I am not talking about your specific warm up that your particular discipline may require, which is a separate thing, just something to keep the freedom that all performers need. BOSS IT!

A special word on depersonalisation.[6,7]

Depersonalisation is that feeling some people get of 'not really being there', or a feeling of unreality. It is probably the parasympathetic nervous system going into override, trying to combat the effects of adrenaline. You might think 'oh, I'm not nervous, I feel divorced from all of this'. But if you are not 'present', how can you give of your best?

If you experience depersonalisation, doing the same techniques can still help by giving it less adrenaline to fight against and restore balance to the whole system. The above measures, and the ones in the next section, on breathing can reduce the build-up of tension, especially if they are done early on.

CHAPTER SIX

Breathe!

The way we breathe can be affected by performance anxiety, through adrenaline. But taking control of our breathing can also be a marvellous way to combat the physical effects of performance anxiety.

Although you may feel like you can't get enough breath, in fact you are highly likely, when your breathing is affected, to be over-breathing. That's known as hyperventilation. This rarely looks like the huffing and puffing we do after vigorous exercise, but is much more subtle. Hence our tendency to misunderstand the signals that our bodies give us. In full blown panic, hyperventilation is usually obvious, but more often it is less easy to spot.

What tends to happen with anxiety is that breathing speeds up, but not obviously. This can go on for much longer periods than people realise. In fact, if you are stressed, or even just thinking about an upcoming event a few days or weeks earlier, this phenomenon can start to kick in then, without you even realising. Then as the performance gets nearer, and even more, on the day, the symptoms might become more severe.

Our bodies operate using a balance in the blood stream of oxygen, that we take in, and carbon dioxide, that we make in the body as a result of activity. Any excess carbon dioxide is blown off during breathing out, but if too much carbon dioxide is lost, that upsets the chemical balance of the body.

Losing too much carbon dioxide can happen because of the inappropriate hyperventilation we are talking about. You see, it would be appropriate to have fast, deep breathing if we were doing something vigorous like running or fighting, since we would be using a lot of energy. But, if we are just thinking, waiting for the game to start and being nervous or stressed, we are not making enough carbon dioxide to warrant that much breathing.

When you are nervous, as well as feeling that you are lacking breath, your breath might feel shallow no matter how deep a breath you try and take, or you may notice you are breathing fast. Your breath may feel tense, or locked. In more severe cases, or as the hyperventilation goes on, you may feel a tingling around your mouth or in the fingers or toes. In severe cases, people can feel dizzy or even faint. The good news is that you can prevent this with corrective breathing (see below). Yes, you can BOSS YOUR BREATHING!

CORRECTIVE BREATHING

The most useful corrective breathing is done before the performance, and ideally regularly in the days leading up to it. This kind of breathing has been studied by biofeedback experts, and you will notice that it is very similar to yogic or meditation or mindfulness breathing. There are probably many similar breathing patterns, with slowed exhalation that can do a similar job[8], but the basics of this one was taught to me at a lecture by biofeedback expert Paul Lehrer[9], and I have found it to be effective and safe.

1. Ideally, find a comfortable place to sit, with your back well supported, and place your hand on your lower tummy. (This can also be done lying down, so long as you are comfortable and warm). Don't attempt this during exercise or whilst doing something else needing your attention, like driving!

2. Try and direct your breath down to your lower tummy *(below the navel). Your abdomen should move out (away from your backbone) when you breathe in and fall back when you breathe out.

If you are very tense, you may find this difficult as the breath may want to lock in the upper chest. In that case, put your hand on your breastbone with slight pressure and mentally instruct it not to rise. The breath will have to go elsewhere.

3. Once you have the pattern of breathing right, you need to
Breathe IN for 3 seconds, and Breathe OUT for 7 seconds

The counts need to be at least as slow as proper seconds, so for best results use a visible timekeeper to check the speed. It is important that your breaths are normal in size, rather than overly big breaths. This can be difficult to achieve at first, so if you have breathed out (or in) as far as you normally would, but still have counts left over, don't keep pushing the air in either direction. Just wait 'still' until the end of that count and then proceed.

Keep doing that for 10-15 minutes.

This is the sort of thing that you need to practise regularly. It's not quite so effective if you do it for the first time just before the performance. If you are especially wound up, or regularly feel tense, do it three times a day at least, especially in the run up to the performance.

Done well, it can bring your pulse rate down, reduce feelings of panic, and help to correct all the adverse effects of adrenaline, allowing the nervous system to come back into balance. It can even help to lower blood pressure.

Once you are used to doing it, it can be very helpful in more immediate situations, like while you are waiting around backstage, for instance.

Technical point: The actual air doesn't go to your lower abdomen, but the muscles here need to relax enough for the diaphragm to be able to move freely, so thinking you are 'breathing to' your lower tummy helps that relaxation of the correct muscles.

If you do feel severe or prolonged tingling around the mouth, giddiness or feel faint, sit down, and try re-breathing into a paper bag, placed over mouth and nose. This can help by increasing carbon dioxide levels appropriately. NOTE: Obviously, you should seek some medical attention if you feel like you might pass out, or if symptoms are severe, prolonged, or happening frequently at times unrelated to performing,   just to confirm what is happening, and to be supervised.

> Little simple short cuts:
>
> These may not be quite as powerful as the full monty just described, but are still helpful:

- In the performance itself, remember the words of Carola Grindea[10], who was a pioneer in terms of understanding Tension in Performance, 'exhalation is your greatest friend'.

In other words, if you feel tense or out of breath, breathe OUT. Strange, but it really can help!!

- Breathe in slowly for 4, hold it for 2, breathe out slowly for 4.

- Yawn!

Mind Control

YOU CAN CONTROL YOUR THOUGHTS!

In fact, in life, sometimes our thoughts are the only thing we can control! You may be surprised at this concept, but it really is in your power. Think about it. At all times, it is the mind that is the initiator for our actions and responses. What's important is how we decide to approach the situation.

Let's go into a bit more depth into those thought processes that can get in the way or that can set off the whole fight or flight response. Then we can look at things in a way that will help us.

CHAPTER SEVEN
What do they really,
really want?

Remember *YOU* are the one *doing something*, but oddly, performance anxiety can make us feel like the audience is there to 'do' something to us!!

Put yourself up in front of an audience and you can feel that it's like saying 'everyone has a right to comment on me'. It's easy to feel you are going to be judged. And there's no getting away from the fact that people are going to have thoughts and feelings about what you do. But is that so bad?

Let's take a look and see what the situation really is......

Think back to when you decided to go and see a play, a concert, a ballet, an opera, a stand-up show, a sports event, or something similar. Why did you go? What were you hoping to do when you got there? Did you go to spot the mistakes? Or were you rooting for the performers to do their best? You may have noticed some mistakes, yes, but that wasn't your focus, and you probably didn't even care about them. Did you go to negatively laugh at the performer? Of course you didn't! Chances are, you were going to enjoy yourself, to be entertained and join in the thrills of live performance. Well, it'll be no surprise to you then, that your audience is there for the same thing. They really are on your side.

OK, OK, let's admit it, in the words of a great friend who performs all around the world: 'There's always one!'.

What she meant is, that there are a very few sad or embittered people out there who think they enjoy putting people down. But really, those are very few and frankly, you're not performing for them. Why would you?! Just ignore them and concentrate on the multi mega majority who are there to enjoy what you do.

As an examiner from the international music exam board ABRSM said to me once "There's nothing better than to be able to just sit back and enjoy an examinee's performance". Yes, even an assessor is there to enjoy him/herself when possible, and the more you can treat any similar 'test' as a performance to be enjoyed by its audience – and you - the better.

A special word for politicians and controversial speakers. This is, of course a little different. Possibly some will be there to criticise, already partisan and unwavering. Well, you are not really there to speak to them either, are you? You can't do anything about them. They have made up their minds, and it doesn't matter what you say. So, they can be mentally ignored by you. Those already on your side are there rooting for you anyway, and those who could sway either way really, really want to hear what you have to say, to help them with their views. If you believe in your message, don't be afraid to speak it from the heart!

A technique that some people like is to imagine the audience either naked, or with ridiculous hairstyles, or with dummies in their mouths etc etc. If it works for you, it'll make you smile inside and take their imagined scary power away.

CHAPTER EIGHT

But am I the best?
Or will I let people down?

You're worried that you're not the best out there. Or maybe a new producer or agent has given you a chance, and you are terrified that you will let them or the company down.

Think of one of your favourite artists, whom you think is the best performer. Does everyone in the world think that that person is the best? Of course not! Everyone has a different opinion, taste, and experience. And that is OK. It doesn't mean they won't enjoy somebody else sometimes. Even our favourite meal all the time would be boring, and we'd be desperate for a new flavour.

And so it is with performers. Give up worrying whether you are 'the best' or not. That is only a matter of individual opinion. Also, whoever is at their best today cannot remain best forever. Whether that's you or anyone else, it's a fact, so get over it! Similarly, when you were hired, you were hired for what you could bring, and the only tool you have is yourself and what you can do.

You can only give what you can give on *that day* at *that time* and in that place. It's a fact. You can do no different. And no amount of worrying whether you are good enough or not, or hoping or praying you are any different will change that fact. You are you at that moment. Full stop. So quit worrying whether that is good, better or best compared to someone else, or whether you'll do it as well or better than last time, or whatever. You do your performance in that moment with the best intentions, and it'll come out how it will come, as only you can do, because you are you.

CHAPTER NINE

It's a gift

I'm not talking about your amazing talent here. I am talking about why on earth you wanted to perform in the first place. Why not just perform in your bedroom, dance to a record in your living room, run around your nearest field, or talk to the wall? Why do you want to do it in front of anybody else?

Could it be that you have something to share? A wish to touch people's hearts in some way?

When you have received a birthday present, you have probably had one of a few reactions; 'Oh, that's amazing, thank you!' (i.e. just what I wanted, better than I dreamed) or 'Very nice, thank you' (i.e. I've got something like that already, but I'll enjoy it sometime), or 'How thoughtful, thank you' (i.e. Well, not sure I'll be able to use that, but it was nice of you to make the effort).

In other words, when someone gives you a present, mostly you will like it to varying degrees. Occasionally you may not like the actual gift, but you will appreciate the fact that someone has taken the trouble of giving it to you.

And that's how it is with a performance. Some people will love it, some will enjoy it very much, and others will think it's maybe not be what they'd have chosen, but they really appreciate the effort that's gone into that. That's life, and you might as well accept that you are not going to be everyone's flavour, even at the highest level.

But you are giving a gift, with your heart and soul, and that will always be appreciated. So do revisit why you really want to perform. That instinct to perform, to give some thing comes deep from within. All you can do is give it.

CHAPTER TEN

Stop catastrophising..........
And then look catastrophe
in the face.

Take a good hard look at the things you are worried about. Forgetting your lines, your steps, the music, where to go, what to do? You might fall over, you might forget the way to the stage, you might forget everything you've been practising, you might rip your suit, you might, you might, you might.

Firstly, just ask yourself, really, what are the chances? If the chances are as rare as hen's teeth, well you can forget about them. Take some time in thought over this if you are disturbed by the 'what ifs'. It's important to get a realistic perspective on your thoughts.

If you have been doing something over and over in a reliable way, the chances of its going wrong during the event are pretty tiny, and on that random occasion, your recovery will most likely be swift and barely noticeable to most. If the chances are quite high because you haven't managed to create or land in the ideal conditions, well, you had better just accept the fact and be prepared to deal with it if it happens.

In sport, people often mess up and sometimes it may even cost the game. But generally, it doesn't kill them and usually doesn't even damage their careers too much. In fact, looking back on a career, it's often seen by them as something they learned and grew from, coming back stronger, and in many cases endeared them to the public.

There are many, many instances of famous performers going wrong. It didn't harm them. Sometimes the opposite. The famous recording of 'Mack the Knife' by Ella Fitzgerald in 1960, Berlin when she forgot the words, and improvised has become a firm favourite because of the brilliant result.

◦ Facing up to those situations:

A great way to help how you feel about potential mistakes is to face them up! NOT in the immediate run up to the performance, but earlier on in the whole process of preparation.

Take the worst kind of mistakes that you worry about and decide and even practise what you would do if it were to happen. A frightening thought! But you'll find it a lot less frightening if you've mentally been through what you would do if it happened, because you'll already have survived it!

◦ Here are some examples:

What are you going to do if you forget the words? Improvise! Make stuff up that makes sense, or gives the gist of what's happening, until you are back on track. You've done your practice. Sooner or later that automatic will kick back, in and take over again. But if you have practised improvising when you make an error, that'll make you feel more comfortable while you're waiting.

What if I forget the next bit of music? Perfect cadence and carry on, is the advice that I heard given to a group of student pianists by their professor.

If you can feel your voice disappearing for an upcoming note, just open your mouth, look happy, and pretend it came out brilliantly! Then continue.

How would you react? What would you do to minimise it for the audience and give them the best possible experience in the circumstances? After all, that's your job, isn't it?

You'll be able to think of all kinds of approaches, but the main thing to do is go over that scary scenario in your mind and realise you can survive it. Sometimes you may think that the best thing to do is just hold your hands up, acknowledge that everything's gone wrong and laugh! It happens, because stuff happens!

By the way, if you catastrophise about things like the building falling down, there's nothing you can do about that, so re-focus immediately! More of that later!

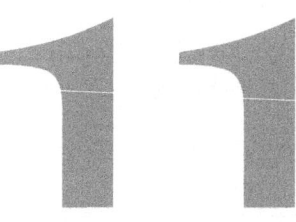

CHAPTER ELEVEN
Stop talking to yourself!

So what's the conversation that goes on in your head?

'I don't feel quite right today'

'I really should have done more practice'

'I shouldn't have had that baguette for lunch'

'Wish I'd got here earlier'

'Oh God, it's critics tonight'

'I can see mum and dad in the second row'

'That was a rather good note'

'That was an awful sound'

'Never managed that so well before'

'What? I've never stumbled over that bit before'

'Love this dress'

'This suit is too tight nowadays!'

Whether it's positive or negative, unintended chatter in your head is distracting you from your performance, so you need to shut it up! [11, 12]

> As I mentioned before, you really can choose
> your thoughts. Try these:

• Exercise 1:

Do a run of your performance, or part of it, and raise your arms up every time you get an unintended thought (positive or negative). This can highlight to you just how often it happens, and what is going on in that head of yours. It works even better if you have someone to perform to during this exercise.

• Exercise 2:

Get lots of your usual internal chatter and put it on a recording. Alternatively, have a friend play the role of your internal chatterer and furnish said friend with your typical powerful distracting thoughts, and invite them to make up a few.

Then run through some of your performance whilst having this chatter played or said into your ear. After a while, chances are that you will either want to throw the recording/ your friend out of the window, or will actually tell them to shut it, or will start to blank them.

At first, you'll probably find it 'paralyses' you, or just makes you agitated. After a while, or after a few goes, like the other distractions, you can become comfortable ignoring them, and re-focusing. You really will be able to decide.

12

CHAPTER TWELVE
Other people's chatter

Some people, or some conversations are just too good at bringing you down or sowing negative thoughts. Some people will not believe in what you do or are trying to do, for reasons that are usually their own. Usually, they are just people who are over cautious, or are just glass half empty people. It isn't even to do with you a lot of the time, but even people who think they are 'looking after you' can have this effect.

Over time, just observe how you feel about yourself and your performing after you have been talking with different people. You will soon know the people who make you feel bad. Be honest with yourself about the effect they are having on you. Then take action. You need to avoid them, or at least avoid these subjects when near them. Don't compromise on this one. Give them a wide berth. DON'T ever hang about and try and make them feel bad. That would still mean you are thinking negatively. And it's not nice!

OK, occasionally you can go round the corner and sound off at them in your own company, just to get it out of your system, but then let it go to the wind. Never hang on to it, as you will be hanging on to a negative.

You need to stay on the positive side with everybody and everything, for your own sake.

Sometimes other people's nervousness can be challenging to be around. Just be aware that these features are theirs, not yours. If you need to, walk away for a while for it not to 'rub off'. Or, when you get good at rechannelling that adrenaline, use their excess energy to funnel into excitement all your own.

A marvellous performer and great friend of mine recently wrote:

> *I like to try and re-define/re-translate anything resembling nerves as sheer excitement. So instead of thinking I'm fearful, I just tell myself I absolutely can't wait to do the gig! This helps keep a lid on adrenaline .... like bees happily in a hive rather than going out to sting people! I find the factors that might loosen that all important lid could be things like total exhaustion, not knowing the piece well enough or inadvertently catching the waves of neuroses of others. Over time I've started to learn quickly how to recognise that tendency in colleagues and shore up my mental defences accordingly.*

PEAK PERFORMANCE

The scope of this book isn't really about all aspects of achieving peak performance, but of course bossing those nerves and achieving peak performance are intimately related, so I must touch on those areas where they come together. Part of it involves giving yourself the best conditions, including keeping a good diet, good hydration, plenty of rest, regular exercise, and on the day, arriving in good time, so that you do not feel rushed. However, I'd like to hone in on a couple of particular points.

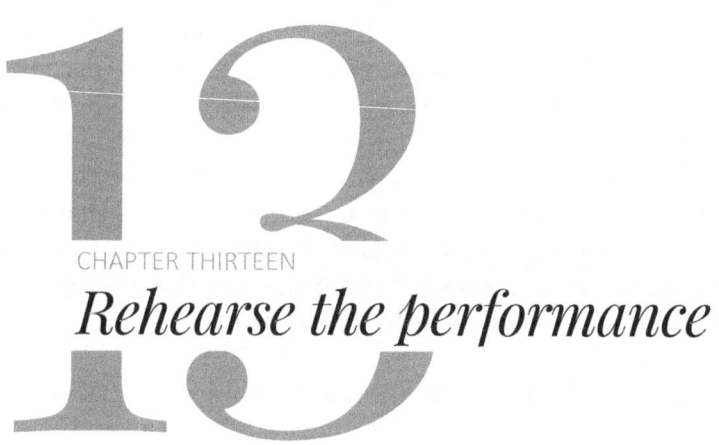

CHAPTER THIRTEEN
Rehearse the performance

Sounds obvious, no? But on the whole, we spend most of the time practising practice!

So you need to imagine the venue. Go there ahead of the performance if you can, to have a look around, but if you can't you need to imagine.

Plan how you will get there in good time. How will you feel when you arrive?

Visualise how it is laid out, how big it is, where you will come in and leave from, where the audience is in relation to you, what the dressing room is like. What's the temperature? How is the lighting? What are you wearing? Where are your refreshments? Are there any? Where are your colleagues? Who is in the audience? Imagine the people you'd most like to be there. Imagine the ones you'd least like to be there. If you are travelling around, you can visualise venues that look different and are of differing sizes. Really try and put detail in. Again, if you don't know for sure all these things, then it is of great value to visualise different versions.

Then do a physical walk in and bow/warm-up/whatever you will do as you enter. Briskly, efficiently, with an audience-loving demeanour! Smiling! Maybe, if you're a boxer you want to strut your stuff in a hard man/woman act. I wouldn't advise that in most situations though!

If you're shy of that bit, remember that your bow or greeting is there to welcome the audience, and say thank you for coming! If you shuffle in looking sheepish, you'll put them on edge. So, walk confidently and give them some love!

Then practise your performance (mentally or physically) with awareness of the audience. Some of them look happy, some look miserable, some are asleep perhaps! (By the way, you can never tell whether an audience member is enjoying it by the way they look!). Where will you look? When do you switch into character? If you're a musician, do you speak? How will you get your music on? What will you say? Every detail. Imagine it, go through it. If you're a sportsman, where's your equipment, coach, towel, water? Who are the other runners or drivers next to you? Which lane are you in?

And at the end of your performance, practise that bow or victory circuit, like it's been the best performance in the world ever! Acknowledge your colleagues or competitors. And walk off, head held high. Oh, and on the actual day, make sure you do it the same way – whatever happened!

It is amazing the confidence it can give you if you have been through that great performance in your head beforehand.

CHAPTER FOURTEEN

A physical pick-me-up for confidence

If you see someone who is feeling down, or shy or uncertain, it sometimes shows in their posture. They may appear slouched, or with shoulders down, hunched over – almost as if they are trying to shrink. Similarly, someone feeling confident and open often shows it in their posture as well.

It might surprise you to find that if you take up a confident posture, you can begin to feel more confident too!

Try walking across the room with shoulders down, head drooping a little, and chest collapsed inwards. Exaggerate it by walking a bit hesitantly with narrow steps. How does it make you feel? Most people start to experience the negative effects straight away.

There are lots of good articles and books on achieving great posture, but I want to point out a couple of useful elements that really seem to help with confidence.

1. Firstly imagine a string arising from the crown of your head that will pull you up all the time in a flexible way.

2. Stretch your arms above your head, fairly close to your ears, with palms facing inwards. Take care not to arch your back at the same time. Pay some attention to the breastbone (sternum), as you do this. You will notice that it rises.

3. Keeping your arms stretched, bring them out to the sides, with palms down, as though you are trying to touch the walls with your fingertips. You will notice that the breastbone falls just a little.

4. Now, using your mind, try and keep that breastbone in the same place as you gradually lower your arms.

5. Now try walking around or saying a few words while maintaining that same posture. How do you feel?

At first it can seem very odd and a bit stiff, but after doing this exercise several times, keeping the shoulders and chest more open usually makes people feel more confident. Some also describe it as a feeling of being ready to give or receive.

Try going about your daily activities like that and see if you can feel a difference.

You can use this technique as an instant 'pick-me-up' whenever you are feeling underconfident.

CHAPTER FIFTEEN
Focus!

One of the greatest tools of all against those distracting and negative thoughts is focus.
The greatest tool in continuing to a great performance after any kind of mishap is focus.

But in order to learn focus, you must know what to focus on. This depends on your specific task, your particular art form, or your sport. So as part of your preparation, using all your knowledge and any guidance you may have, you must really, really discover what it is you need to focus on, both in terms of the whole performance, and at any point in time.

I am a singer, so I shall talk about that. My overall aim is to convey the music as embodiment of the character with the best and most appropriate tone and physicality that I can make, in ensemble with whatever instruments or other singers that are involved. Ideally, for peak performance, I can just immerse myself in the character, and what the character is 'saying' or doing at that moment. But underpinning that is technique and knowledge of the piece. Again, how to best get into character is the scope of a different book.

But the point is, you need to learn what your focus is going to be when you begin. Then you can let anything else just be there, and not interfere with it.

If anything happens during the performance (and in a whole opera plenty does!) to throw me off balance, then I immediately focus hard on what I have to do to make the next bit come good, be that technical, interpretive or interactive, and get back into that immersive interpretation as soon as possible.

Whatever has gone wrong has past, your job is to focus on what comes next, not to focus on what anyone else might think about it, or how bad you think it was. You have put so much into this and you really can trust to all that hard work.

It is important to be aware what is around you when you perform (after all a colleague may go wrong, and you may have to adapt- something else you can practise, and is definitely worth doing if you have a colleague who is not so sure of themselves). If you cut yourself off, you won't come across as authentic, nor with any presence. However, that's not the same as remaining focussed, which is your aim.

CHAPTER SIXTEEN

When performance anxiety isn't performance anxiety

Sometimes people experience the features of performance anxiety at times other than during the performance. They may be heightened on performance day, but they are present a lot of the time in other situations. If that is the case with you, then there may be a deeper psychological issue that you need to look at, and I'd advise you seek some additional professional input for that, maybe from a doctor or a psychologist.

In a few performers, it can be a sign that deep down they don't want to be doing this at all. Maybe performing is something that their family or teachers guided them into just because they were good at their art or sport, and everyone, including them just assumed that this is what they were supposed to do in life.

I believe that it never does anyone any harm in any walk of life to truly look deep into their heart to ask themselves the question 'do I really want to be on this path?'. It may take a little time, and the process can scare you quite a bit, but afterwards, you will be so much more secure in what you are doing. You'll also realise that if you want to do this, then you may as well forget worrying about how good you are at it. So long as you are striving for your best, you know you are worthy of giving it a shot. It's your destiny!

AND FINALLY.....

Remember to CELEBRATE and HAVE FUN! You can practise that too!! Seriously, it's important. When you do something good in practice, cheer, leap, hurrah and reward yourself. It's the GOOD experiences we want to remember, so make sure you give those bits plenty of attention too. Then they'll happen more and more often.

References:

1. Music, Motor Control and the Brain. 2006, p. 313. Edited by Eckart Altenmüller, Mario Wiesendanger, and Jurg Kesselring. ISBD-13: 978-0198530008. OUP Oxford

2. https://www.youtube.com/watch?v=qU7R1woaNF0 Ella Fitzgerald

3. https://www.thisisanfield.com/2020/10/i-get-nervous-too-jurgen-klopps-touchinletter-to-young-lfc-fan-struggling-with-anxiety/

4. Neuropsychology and Performance Anxiety – Priyanka Potdar- TED Talk https://youtu.be/TswQDR1byIQ

5. The Secrets of Performing Confidence. 2003, p. 102-3 by Evans, Andrew ISBN: 0-7136-6288-3. A&C Black. London

6. Hunter ECM, Sierra M, David AS. The epidemiology of depersonalisation and derealisation: a systematic review. Social Psychiatry and Psychiatric Epidemiology. 2004; 39:9–18. doi: 10.1007/s00127-004-0701-4

7. Depersonalization Experiences in Undergraduates Are Related to Heightened Stress Cortisol Responses. Giesbrecht, Timo; Smeets, Tom Merckelbach, Harald; Jelicic, Marko. The Journal of Nervous and Mental Disease: April 2007 - Volume 195 - Issue 4 - p 282-287

8. Front. Hum. Neurosci., 07 September 2018: How Breath-Control Can Change Your Life: A Systematic Review on Psycho-Physiological Correlates of Slow Breathing. A. Zacarro, A. Piarulli, M. Laurino, E. Garbell, D. Menicucci, B. Neri and A. Gemignani.

9. Principles and Practice of Stress Management, Third Edition 2008. Paul M. Lehrer, Robert L. Woolfolk, et al. ISBN-13: 978-1606230008. Guilford Press

10. Tensions in the Performance of Music: a symposium edited by Carola Grindea; foreword by Yehudi Menuhin; preface by Allen Percival. 1995 ISBN: 1-871082-59-5. Kahn and Averill.

11. The Inner Game of Tennis: The Ultimate Guide to the Mental Side of Peak Performance. 2015 by W Timothy Gallwey. ISBN-13 : 978-1447288503 Pan; Main Market edition.

12. Creating Confidence. 1999 by Bunch, Meribeth. ISBN: 0-7494-2782-5 Kogan Page.

Made in the USA
Middletown, DE
12 July 2023